My Healing Journey

By
Shawnmica Townsend

My Healing Journey

Copyright © 2024 Shawnmica Townsend

All rights reserved. No part of this book may be reproduced, distributed, or transmitted in any form or by any means without the prior consent of written permitted of the author, except in the case of brief quotes used in reviews.

This book is dedicated to the ones who have lost their way dealing with any form of hardship. To the ones that are struggling to let go of unhealthy situations. To the ones who always give more than they should. I pray that you find your inner strength and regain your power back.

Fueled

When I was able to turn my pain into passion it fueled my soul. My pain started to pour out and words formed. I realized I had so much to say.

Release

I asked God to save me from me. To help release this beautiful soul that's within. Help me to open up my mind so I can see a clearer view. I've been hidden within my shadow for way too long. So long that I don't recognize me. I've let pain and hurt consume me. I'm ready to step into the light and shine. Shine like the beautiful diamond God created me to be.

Within

Beauty comes from within. I'm loving myself from the inside out. I love feeding my soul with positivity, watering my self-worth.

Evolving

Evolving is what I'm focusing on moving forward. My time is now. I feel things about to fall into place for me. I'm creating spaces in my life for my upcoming blessings. I'm truly walking into my purpose.

Healing

I had to pull myself out of a dark place. I had to stop hiding and face the things that were happening around me. I had to take it all in at once. It's been a journey, but I'm healing here.

Wiser

I've made a lot of progress over the years. I've come a long way manifesting things I set out to achieve. I'm proud of myself for not giving up. I had a lot of setbacks, but my come back will be powerful. The reason being is because with a clearer mindset I am now wiser.

Refreshing

There are parts of me that are still in the making. Taking time out for me. Taking time out to restore myself. This new version of me feels refreshing. I'm loving the way things are starting to unfold.

Reward

I'm preparing for a better me. I'm onto something new. Opening minds and exploring thoughts. This is my becoming season and I'm embracing it. It took me a while to get where I'm at, but I'm here. So, every reward that comes my way just know I've earned it.

Bloom

In a world that is unsteady, hold your balance and never lose focus. There are no limitations on the things that you can accomplish. Even if you have to take it slow. It's okay, even flowers take time to bloom.

Rise

Never doubt yourself, not even for a second. You can do anything that you put your whole heart into. This world is full of people who wants to kill your passion. Rise above it all and show the world who you are. Remember when you do it make sure you are doing it with no apologies and with no regrets. Whenever you are feeling uninspired nourish yourself back to health. Remind yourself just how amazing you are.

Ease

When you are around someone and your body feels at ease, that is a beautiful moment to be in. When they feel like a breath of fresh air. You can just feel their positive energy all around you. Those people you want to hold onto, because they were heaven sent. God sent them to you on purpose.

Growth

I love looking in the mirror and loving what I see. Choosing growth over comfort. I was in my comfort zone for way too long. Afraid to step out into the world and explore. I owe the world an apology, for not cherishing this beautiful thing we call life.

Wholly

I'm at a point in my life where I want to be loved wholly. Not partially and not in-between. I want to be loved correctly or leave me be completely.

LIGHTER

I'm learning to let go and let God. When
I tell you by letting go of some of that hurt
and anger it lifted my heart. In a way that I
didn't even think was possible. I'm learning
to accept things for what they are. You cannot
control things that are out of your control. That
burden I was carrying was getting to be too heavy
to hold onto. Now when I walk it feels like I'm
floating. My heart just feels lighter.

Freed

When I started loving me more, I stopped feeling like a prisoner. I slowly began restoring myself. Doing the things that made me happy. That kept me smiling. That brought out that beautiful glow in me. The shackles were finally off, I freed myself from the inside out.

Role

When I give I intent to give way too much. I am currently working on not giving so much of me to people. Learning to know my role when it's being presented to me. Making sure that I don't overplay my part.

Storm

I couldn't see it before, but I can see it now. Things happen for a reason, and it's up to you to determine the outcome of it. It's either you are going to weather the storm or soak in it. You have to face the tough reality, and that's nobody is coming to save you, but you.

Envision

Your journey awaits for you. Envision the kind of life you want to seek and go for it. I'm not saying it's going to be that simple or a smooth sailing. Of course, there will be difficulties along the way. Nothing comes easily to most people. In life you must put in the work. It starts with putting one foot in front of the other.

Mindset

This growth feels different probably because my mindset is different. I try to avoid things that would get me out my hook up. Things that would tarnish my character. I'm not doing the back and forth with no one. Nowadays my tolerance level is low. To protect my peace, I'll let you feel like you have the upper hand. Leaving you where you're at.

Peace

Having inner peace feels amazing to the point that it even feels powerful. I love the type of love that I'm developing for myself. Being able to let go of damaging situations, and just enjoy the peace of mind that comes from it.

Speak

I hope this speaks to your heart and reaches your beautiful soul. Always do what's best for you no matter what. Don't stay in a situation where you feel it's not serving you anymore. Where you are being unseen. When something no longer serves you cut ties. Go where you are constantly celebrated and where you are clearly seen.

Leap

I am ready to take that leap of faith. I'm done waiting to see what's going to happen next. I'm ready to manifest the type of life that I've been praying for. Anything that makes me happy I'm doing it. Designing my own life, my own happiness.

Instilled

No one has the power to shatter what's already instilled in me. I don't know what the future will bring, but I know that everything that is currently happening to me was set in place. It was already aligned for me.

Free

Give yourself the okay, to just be.
Be free of all the things that's holding
you back from you reaching your full
potential. Fall in love with taking care
of you first. Everything else is secondary.

Focus

Keep the focus on you. Don't worry about what's swarming around you. It's only purpose is to knock you off your game. Keep your eyes fixed. Zoom in and lock in on your purpose.

Win

I am so addicted to bettering myself that I think about it, speak about it, dream about it, and even write my vision and goals down. You see this is how you manifest things that you want. You have to put it out there. Put it into the atmosphere. I already know my time is coming. My heart is too kind and pure not to win in life.

Time

It took me a while to realize just how precious time is. What can I say I'm a late bloomer. I always felt that time was on my side. I got a lot of catching up to do. I cannot afford to waste any more time. I only want to surround myself with people who influence my thoughts and inspire me to be and do better.

Aura

I try to start my day off with good
intentions. When I get up in the
morning, I cleanse myself. I speak
positive affirmations to myself. I
look in the mirror and in admiration
I smile. I love being in this aura, self-love.

Stacked

Every problem I have I'm counting my blessings. No matter if the odds are stacked against me. I'm betting on myself every time. I know in my heart that no matter where my feet are planted, it's a sure thing I will bloom. You see when God is ready for you to grow he will water you.

Fasting

I have been fasting not just physically, but mentally as well. Fasting from people who are no longer moving in the same direction as me. Anything that's hindering my growth I'm at peace with setting it free.

Calm

At times when I go ghost know that it is a me thing. People judge and see it as a red flag. But if you know me then you know. When my energy is off I go into isolation. When I isolate myself from others, it helps to heal parts of me. I can't quite put my finger on it, but it helps to relax my mind and calm my soul.

Spaces

I had to take accountability for how people were treating me. Allowing them to fill up spaces that they outgrew. By me being a good hearted person people took advantage of that. I had to sit back and reevaluate what was important to me. I had to create boundaries for my own well-being.

Watch

When you start to live your life the way you want to live it, just watch how you start to glow differently. Watch how small your circle becomes. Watch how your mind just opens up. Watch how the universe starts moving things around in your favor. Just watch.

Revealing

No longer will I postpone my self-care to attend to other people needs and wants. No one is entitled to the time I set aside for myself. Every day as I walk forward I smile. Because I love revealing parts of me that's being awakened.

Trusting

My path is much smoother now, because my focus shifted. I truly feel that there is something special out there just waiting for me to claim. I feel like I'm entering into the trusting phase in my life. Trusting that if I put God first the rest will soon fall into place.

Energy

The energy I've been giving off is different nowadays. I'm no longer that "yes" girl. I was always catering to others needs before my own. Those days are gone and are over with. I am standing on business now. My no's means no. I am proud of myself because now I put me first. And I love that for me.

Lifecycle

No one should have so much power that it breaks your focus. I know we all get lost sometimes with life itself. Try not to lose sight of the importance and that's living. Years could easily go by and before you know it life done passed right by you. Don't waste your lifecycle. Instead follow all your dreams and every thought that crosses your mind. Hey, even the crazy ones that makes you chuckle.

Courage

Sometimes I have to put my life on DND (Do Not Disturb) for my own well-being. Glorifying my needs and space to self-reflect. I found courage to manifest a new outcome. Normalizing removing myself from unhealthy vibes.

Rare

People often say "Kill them with kindness."
I'll rather kill them with my absence. When
it comes to me I'm rare. You don't get two
of me in one lifetime. So, if you ever fumbled
me just take that lost and learn from it.

Self

Dear self, I am loving the woman that you are becoming. Everything that you do make sure, that you are doing it for you. Give it everything you got and then give it a little more. Let there be no room for doubts.

Shaped

Day by day I am being shaped into someone I am proud to be. Learning and relearning things about myself. It's okay to shift your energy to challenge your growth. Surpass what you think are your limits. Go further than what you did yesterday.

Flex

A real flex is when you're comfortable in your own skin. When you are being exactly who you are. Without any care or validation. Loving who you are no matter what you're enduring.

Authentic

The love I give off can't be duplicated. It's authentic. I'm going to be the best version of myself every single time. Loving myself unconditionally and blocking out things that don't align with me.

Motion

My problem is that I'm too loyal to the wrong souls. There will be no more energy being sucked out of me. If you're not pouring into me with the same motion that I'm pouring into you, your access will be denied.

Scars

I wear a lot of scars that are unseen. Each scar taught me a lesson. Acknowledging and accepting things for what they are. Pain changed my perspective on life. It released me to be exactly who I needed to be.

Notice

When it comes to negative energy I just can't vibe with that kind of mindset. Take notice, I'm no longer giving people the benefit of the doubt. If you played your hand with me be prepared for the aftermath. The truth is you won't get the same me twice.

Piecing

I'm on a different type of time. Piecing back the broken parts of me. Taking back my power. When you start to realize who you are you won't tolerate certain things. Life becomes healthier when you eliminate waste.

Queen

I'm not forcing anything anymore.
I'm not watering nothing that doesn't
grow. That doesn't flourish. I have no
desire to convince anyone to be in my life.
When I decide to walk away, it's because
I'm choosing me. I'm protecting me.
Respecting the Queen in me.

Clarity

When the energy changes I'm no longer waiting to see if the energy is going to shift back in my favor. I'm going to simply ask for clarity. I'm on a need to know basis. You don't have to sugar code anything when it comes to me. Keep it real, it's either we're rocking or we're not.

Pace

Your journey is yours, so own it. It doesn't have to match anyone else's. No matter how long it may take you to get to where you need to be. Do whatever works for you, and do it at your own pace. Stay focused and consist. Even if you have to go slow, just stay the course. Remember you can be a tortoise and still win the race.

Owning

Self-love is where it all begins. Owning your own story and creating your own outcome. Knowing that the old you is gone, that version of you is no longer available. So, set free the past you, so that the new you can be released.

Life

When in doubt find the courage, you need to believe in yourself again. Embrace the hand that's been dealt for you. Even if you have to rearrange it make it work for you. Take a second and appreciate where you are now. Hey, you only get one life. So why not make the best of it.

Errors

With my decisions in life I'm finding peace with them. Educating myself from past mistakes. Life is full of red errors, but don't let that define you. Even if you have to start from scratch, just do it.

Vision

My mind is so different from others that its mind blowing. Many don't get what I'm trying to accomplish in this life time. I've been staying out the way, so I can execute my vision. Breaking generational curses.

Watering

I'm letting go of any stress that comes my way. I'm only welcoming in happiness. Watering these seeds of my life. As I'm growing and glowing so beautifully.

Era

I'm so impressed with myself. I'm proud
of every step that I take, that hits the ground.
Shedding dead weight as it falls off me, like
petals from an unwatered flower. As I continue
to strive, I'm finally walking into my era of greatness.

Rebirth

Enjoying my journey and what comes with it, experiencing the in between. The old me that is slowly fading and the new me being rebirth.

Made in the USA
Columbia, SC
18 November 2024